GAL
CENGAGE Learning

Literary Newsmakers for Students, Volume 3

Project Editor: Anne Marie Hacht Rights Acquisition and Management: Scott Bragg, Edna Shy, Jhanay Williams, and Robyn Young Composition: Evi Abou-El-Seoud Manufacturing: Drew Kalasky

Imaging: Lezlie Light

Product Design: Pamela A. E. Galbreath, Jennifer Wahi Content Conversion: Katrina Coach, Civie Green Product Manager: Meggin Condino © 2009 Gale, Cengage Learning

For product information and technology assistance, contact us at **Gale Customer Support, 1-800-877-4253**.

For permission to use material from this text or product, submit all requests online at www.cengage.com/permissions.

Further permissions questions can be emailed to permissionrequest@cengage.com While every effort has been made to ensure the reliability of the information presented in this publication, Gale, a part of Cengage Learning, does not guarantee the accuracy of the data contained herein. Gale accepts no payment for listing; and inclusion in the publication of any organization, agency, institution, publication, service, or individual does not imply endorsement of the editors or publisher. Errors brought to the attention of the publisher and verified to the satisfaction of the publisher will be corrected in future editions.

Gale
27500 Drake Rd.
Farmington Hills, MI, 48331-3535

ISBN-13: 978-1-4144-0280-2
ISBN-10: 1-4144-0280-5
ISSN 1559-9639

This title is also available as an e-book.
ISBN-13: 978-1-4144-3527-5
ISBN-10: 1-4144-3527-4
Contact your Gale, a part of Cengage Learning sales
representative for ordering information.

No Country for Old Men

Cormac McCarthy

2005

Introduction

No Country for Old Men (2005) brings Cormac McCarthy's idiosyncratic syntax and spare dialogue to the crime novel genre. While the book examines the large themes—such as violence and culture clash—that are McCarthy's stock and trade, it uses the basic thriller formula to tell a fast-moving story about an Everyman, a lawman from a different era, and a sociopathic killer.

Like the previous three novels that make up

Cormac McCarthy's border trilogy, *No Country for Old Men* is set along the Texas-Mexico border. It details the effects of a drug deal gone bad in 1980 and allows McCarthy to turn his eye toward the drugs, guns, and issues relating to violence and modernity. Taken from a line in William Butler Yeats's poem "Sailing to Byzantium," the novel's title refers to Sheriff Ed Tom Bell's feelings about the changing times and what people are willing to do to one another in pursuit of money and power. *No Country for Old Men* is a violent book, and McCarthy never shies away from describing murder and mayhem in the most gory detail.

Though the novel shares many of the characteristics of McCarthy's earlier works, it also breaks new ground for the author. On one level it serves as a philosophical meditation on good and evil—as do, for example, the books of the Border Trilogy—but it also features a plot based on the classics of the crime novel genre. In *No Country for Old Men* McCarthy abandons the Western, historical genre for a form of storytelling centered on making his tale a reflection of the modern world.

Author Biography

Born on July 20, 1933, in Rhode Island, Cormac McCarthy published his first novel in 1965. In all, he has published ten books. *The Road* (2006) won the Pulitzer Prize in 2006.

In 1937, when Cormac McCarthy was four years old, his father Charles McCarthy moved his family to Knoxville, Tennessee, where he signed on as a lawyer for the Tennessee Valley Authority. After high school, Cormac went on to the University of Tennessee as a liberal arts major. Beginning in 1953, he served four years with the U.S. Air Force. When his stint in the military ended, he returned to the university and worked on the student newspaper and won the Ingram-Merrill Award for journalism in 1959 and 1960. McCarthy left the University of Tennessee without earning a degree and moved to Chicago with his wife, Lee Holleman, and their son, Cullen.

In 1965 McCarthy published his first novel, *The Orchard Keeper*, with Random House. His editor, Albert Erskine, had served as William Faulkner's editor until Faulkner's death in 1962. This novel and its three successors—*Outer Dark* (1968), *Child of God* (1974), and *Suttree* (1979)— were all set in Appalachia and would establish McCarthy as a writer in the Southern Gothic genre.

During this period, McCarthy won several awards that helped him travel and write. Before *The*

Orchard Keeper was published, he received a fellowship from the American Academy of Arts and Letters. In 1966 he received the Rockefeller Foundation Grant, and three years later, the Guggenheim Fellowship for Creative Writing. This fertile period culminated with his move to El Paso, Texas, and the completion of one of his most highly regarded novels, *Blood Meridian* (1985). With *Blood Meridian* McCarthy moved away from the Southern Gothic style and set his characters in the Southwestern United States. Following the exploits of a gang of scalp hunters, the novel spares no detail in describing the violence of the era along the U.S.–Mexico border in the late 1840s.

The 1990s would see McCarthy deepen his meditation on the Southwestern United States and publish three more novels set along the Rio Grande. Collectively known as the border trilogy, *All the Pretty Horses* (1992), *The Crossing* (1994), and *Cities of the Plain* (1998) follow characters who move through the complex and often dangerous cultures of southern Texas and Mexico.

In the 2000s, McCarthy's growing fame as a writer was matched by his reluctance to enter into the public eye. In 2005 McCarthy published *No Country for Old Men* and followed it with *The Road* (2006) and *The Sunset Limited: A Novel in Dramatic Form*. That year, *The Road* won the Pulitzer Prize for fiction and was chosen as an *Oprah's Book Club* selection. This nudge into the spotlight was helped along by *No Country for Old Men*'s adaptation into a popular film in 2007.

McCarthy has granted only a handful of interviews over the course of his career and carefully guards his privacy. He continues to write and now lives near Santa Fe, New Mexico, with his wife and son.

Plot Summary

No Country for Old Men is a fast-moving story about an ordinary man, Llewelyn Moss, who stumbles on more than two million dollars and then must escape the people he knows are coming to get it back. Spread out over southwest Texas, the hunt for Moss is taken up by Anton Chigurh, a cold and almost preternaturally talented killer for hire. Also searching for Moss are men from the notorious Pablo Acosta's drug-dealing group. The chase also involves Sheriff Ed Tom Bell, an aging lawman who yearns for the simpler "bad guys" of the past. McCarthy takes these basic elements of the crime caper and adds significant twists, leaving the ending far from what the reader might expect.

Moss stumbles onto the carnage of a drug deal gone wrong while hunting antelopes. The remote desert location is littered with bodies and shot-up trucks, one containing a shipment of heroin. After tracking a bloody trail, Moss comes upon the last man. Next to him lies a nearly forty-pound satchel of cash. Moss hesitates; he knows that some very bad people will do very bad things to retrieve the money. He deliberates—but cannot resist. He takes the money and returns home to his baffled wife, Carla Jean, who quizzes him on the satchel and the gun that Moss has taken from one of the dead men. For safety, Moss puts her on a bus to her grandmother's house in Odessa, and he then hits the road, hoping to keep himself alive long enough to figure out how to deal with the money.

On Moss's trail is Anton Chigurh, a character maybe more at home in the slasher genre than in the conventional crime novel. McCarthy introduces Chigurh in the book's first scene. He lets himself be arrested for a moving violation just to see if he can free himself, which he does in the most violent way possible. He slips out of the handcuffs and uses them to garrote the young deputy who brought him to the police station. Chigurh's weapon of choice is a slaughterhouse stun gun powered by a tank of highly compressed air.

One step behind Chigurh (and two steps behind Moss) is Sheriff Ed Tom Bell. He knows that Moss took the money, and he sees the mayhem that Chigurh leaves in his wake. Each chapter of *No Country for Old Men* begins with Bell's interior monologue, each exploring a variation of a theme, namely: this country is going to hell and we are not ready to cope with it. The amoral, almost unbelievably violent Chigurh is the embodiment of the coming evil that Bell senses.

The cat-and-mouse game moves from motel to motel, with Moss trying to outwit his pursuers, which include Chigurh, Bell, and also a Mexican faction charged with recovering the loot. Moss is clever. He hides the money in motel air conditioning ducts and, when he is almost found by his pursuers, he switches rooms and fishes the satchel down through the ducts with some taped-together tent poles.

His flight takes him to a border hotel in Eagle Pass, where he discovers that the satchel has a tracking beacon and that his pursuers can find him easily. Moss now knows that he might have to kill someone in order to keep the money. Soon after Moss discovers the beacon, Chigurh finds him at the hotel. Moss disarms Chigurh and runs. But Chigurh pulls out his secondary gun and wounds Moss with a long-distance shot. Chigurh's pursuit is cut short by the arrival of members of the Mexican gang, and a gunfight between Chigurh and the Mexicans rages as Moss escapes from the area. Bloody and barely able to press on, Moss heaves the satchel over the border bridge and, hoping to recover the money later, crosses into Mexico.

As Moss is healing his wounds in a Mexican hospital, he is visited by Carson Wells, an exmilitary man familiar with Chigurh's bloody resumé. Wells is hired to rein in the uncontrollable Chigurh and warns Moss that he cannot escape such a bloodthirsty, clever killer. Wells offers to put Chigurh off of his pursuit of Moss if he will give the money back. Moss brushes him off, and Wells leaves. Sensing the extent of the danger, Moss calls Carla Jean and convinces her to go into hiding with her grandmother.

Carla Jean is also on Sheriff Bell's mind. After tracking and investigating the multiple crime scenes left behind by the maniacal Chigurh, Bell drives up to see Carla Jean and asks her to tell him where Moss is hiding. But Carla Jean is confident that Moss can outwit and outrun his pursuers and will not give up any information she has about Moss.

Meanwhile, Chigurh has sustained serious injuries from the gun battle in Eagle Pass. He blows up a car in front of a pharmacy in order to sneak in and get the painkillers and antibiotics he needs to recover. He checks into a hotel, stoically dresses his wounds, and hides out for several days to heal. When he does rejoin his hunt for Moss, he is surprised by the beeping of the tracking device. Chigurh tracks the signal to a nearby hotel and discovers, to his surprise, that it is Wells that has the beacon. Chigurh confronts Wells in his hotel room and kills him.

Moss attempts to call Wells only to reach Chigurh, who now has Wells's cell phone. Chigurh tells Moss that unless he gives up the money immediately, Carla Jean will be killed. Moss threatens to stop running and bring the fight right to Chigurh. Moss then checks out of his hotel and returns to the Texas side of the border. At this point, Carla Jean and her grandmother pack up and move to El Paso to be safer.

Moss then rents a cab and recovers the money that he had thrown into the crevass below the border bridge. He pays the cabbie to drive him to San Antonio, where he buys a gun and a truck. On his way back to west Texas, Moss picks up a teenage hitchhiker, a girl he asks to help him drive. Though wary of Moss, she helps him drive and keeps him company.

In the next scene, Carla Jean calls Sheriff Bell

to tell him that Moss has called her and she knows where he is. Bell assures her that he will try to help Moss and she gives him Moss's location. But the line is tapped by Acosta's men and they immediately track down Moss at his motel and kill him, along with the hitchhiker. Bell shows up too late and can only hang his head at the loss of life. Later, Chigurh comes to the motel and breaks into Moss's room late at night. He knows that Moss has hidden the satchel in air ducts before, so he unscrews the grating from the vent. He quickly finds the money. As he gets into his car to leave, Bell pulls up in his police car to have one more look at the crime scene. Chigurh lays back in his car, and Bell never knows that he is there.

Chigurh returns the money to the American drug syndicate and Bell goes to tell Carla Jean that Moss is dead. Shortly afterward, Carla Jean's grandmother dies. After the funeral Chigurh lays in wait for Carla Jean at her home. He tells her that he must keep his oath to kill her, even though the money has been returned and Moss has been killed. Carla Jean cannot comprehend Chigurh's twisted fatalism and begs for her life. He tells her that the past cannot be undone and kills her. Driving away from her house, Chigurh is struck by a car and severely wounded. He limps away from the accident and slings his broken arm with a shirt that he buys from a pair of gawking boys. Chigurh gives the boys money and tells them to forget they ever saw him.

In the novel's denouement, Bell visits his aging

and paralyzed uncle, Ellis, who lives alone outside of town. Throughout the book, Bell's interior monologues show him to be worn down by the changing ways of society. Bell is convinced that the world is growing more and more evil and that he must retire or face becoming evil himself in order to effectively combat it. Bell confesses to his uncle that during his tour of duty in World War II, he felt he abandoned his comrades after an enemy mortar strike blew up the house in which they were hiding. Ellis somewhat absolves the younger Bell by telling him that he has been too hard on himself.

For Bell, not being able to save Moss from Chigurh or the Acosta gang is the final motivation he needs to retire from law enforcement. He feels outmatched by a new breed of criminal, one that has no code, no morals, and no qualms about murdering anyone who stands in their way. Bell's wife is surprised by his decision and tries to reassure him about his effects as a sheriff over the past decades. For Bell, the decision to retire is difficult and settling into his new civilian life proves to be a challenge.

No Country for Old Men ends with one of Bell's interior monologues. In it, he remembers a water trough carved from stone that stood outside the house that was blown up in World War II. With mankind being so violent and almost certainly headed for obliteration, Bell wonders what would have motivated a man to take a hammer and chisel to a solid piece of rock and carve a water trough made to last ten thousand years. He guesses that the man must have had some sort of "promise in his heart." Bell hopes that he can make that kind of promise too.

In the novel's closing paragraphs, Bell recalls a dream that he had about his father. In the dream, Bell and his father are riding horses. They are riding together toward some unknown place in cold and utter darkness. As his father rides ahead of him, Bell sees that the man is carrying and sheltering a small fire. As his father rides into the blackness ahead of him and out of sight, Bell knows that his father has gone ahead to make a fire in all that cold and darkness and that when Bell arrives, his father will be there.

Characters

Ed Tom Bell

Ed Tom Bell is one of the novel's main characters. He is the sheriff of Terrell County, Texas. At the start of each chapter, the reader is privy to his thoughts on his career and life through short, stream-of-consciousness prologues printed in italics. Bell is the quintessential old-timer. He has been sheriff since he was twenty-five and feels the presence of a new evil in the world. Bell and his ilk are the eponymous "old men" in the novel's title. His musings depict his thought process as he comes to the decision that he can no longer function as a lawman in a world of such desperation and violence. Throughout the book, Bell mulls over retiring and how it will affect his life and his wife, Loretta. Toward the end of the novel, he visits his shut-in uncle, Ellis, a former lawman paralyzed by a gunshot. Bell recounts a battle from World War II in which he left his unit after a bombing raid. Though he knows that his fellow soldiers were likely dead, his conscience is weighed down by the memory. This memory informs Bell's moral code; he feels that his life was spared in World War II, and he drives himself to make up for it.

Media Adaptations

- *No Country for Old Men* was adapted as a film by Joel and Ethan Coen in 2007. It is distributed by Miramax Films in the United States and by Paramount Vantage outside of the United States. The film features Tommy Lee Jones as Sheriff Ed Tom Bell; Josh Brolin as Llewelyn Moss; and Javier Bardem as Anton Chigurh.

- *All the Pretty Horses* was released as a film in 2000 and starred Matt Damon as John Grady Cole and Penelope Cruz as Alejandra. The movie was directed by Billy Bob Thornton and released by Miramax Films.

- *All the Pretty Horses* is available as

an unabridged compact disc, published by Harper Audio in 2000 and read by Frank Muller.

- *All the Pretty Horses*, *The Crossing*, and *Cities of the Plain* are also available as an abridged six-cassette set, read by Brad Pitt.

Loretta Bell

Loretta Bell married Ed Tom Bell when she was seventeen. She is a devoted wife and sounding board for her husband as he attempts to sort out the ethical dilemmas of his life and career.

Anton Chigurh

Anton Chigurh is a ruthless killer-for-hire paid to bring back the money that Llewelyn Moss finds at the scene of the drug deal. Chigurh lives by a strict code, and in some ways, is an evil mirror-image of Ed Tom Bell. His fatalist philosophy pushes him along in his pursuit of Moss and the money, and he murders anyone and destroys anything that gets in his way. As he explains to Carla Jean Moss, "Every moment in your life is a turning and every one a choosing. Somewhere you made a choice. All followed to this." For Chigurh, the incredible complexity of human relationships and criss-crossing paths is preordained and makes utter sense, although it may appear random and chaotic. He sees himself and his murderous deeds as simple effects of causes that he did not set in motion. It is this philosophy that supports his bloody sociopathic methods. Chigurh is in top physical form and almost superhuman in his ability to endure and inflict pain. He is adept with whatever weapon is at hand, but prefers to use an air-powered slaughterhouse stun gun. Chigurh engages his soon-to-be victims in discussion about fate, life, and death.

Ellis

Ellis is Ed Tom Bell's uncle. He worked as a deputy with Ed Tom's grandfather, Jack, who was also a sheriff. Ellis was shot in the line of duty and subsequently confined to a wheelchair. With the exception of some half-feral cats, Ellis lives by himself and is resigned to his fate. Toward the end of the novel, Bell goes to visit Ellis and makes a confession. This conversation helps to shed more light on the stream-of-consciousness prologues that open each chapter. During World War II, Bell left his combat unit after a house they were using as shelter was bombed. Though he believed his comrades were dead and that he had no chance to save them, Bell has carried the guilt from this incident throughout his life, and it is this guilt that has sustained his sense of honor and morality. Ellis tries to absolve Bell of his guilt by telling him that he has been too hard on himself and that Bell's nagging conscience is simply a sign of old age.

Girl Hitchhiker

Moss picks up this teenage hitchhiker just before he is shot and killed by the Mexican dealers. He gives her money and buys her dinner in exchange for helping him drive. While she claims that she is on her way to California, Moss is skeptical. He judges her age at around sixteen. Moss and the girl carry on a comfortable but vague conversation, each unwilling to come out and tell the other who they really are and the details of their individual situations. Moss and the girl stop at a motel and Moss rents two rooms. He regards her as a girl in need of help and resists her advances. At this time, Carla Jean Moss calls Bell to tell him that she has talked to Moss and knows where he is. The Mexican dealers have tapped her phone and race to the motel to reclaim the money. Moss, the girl, and one of the dealers die in the ensuing shootout.

Deputy Haskins

Deputy Haskins arrests Chigurh in the opening scene of the novel. Chigurh frees himself from the handcuffs and strangles Haskins to death.

Sheriff Lamar

Sheriff Lamar oversees the police force of Sutton County, Texas. Lamar works with Ed Tom Bell to catch Chigurh. Lamar's officer Deputy Haskins is strangled by Chigurh in the opening scene of the novel.

Carla Jean Moss

Carla Jean married Llewelyn Moss when she was sixteen, and she is nineteen when the events of the novel begin. After he finds the money, Llewelyn sends Carla Jean to stay with her grandmother in Odessa, Texas. When Chigurh talks to Moss on the phone, he tells him that he will kill Carla Jean if the money is not returned instantly. Chigurh keeps this promise; though he murders Moss and recovers the money, Chigurh surprises Carla Jean on the day of her grandmother's funeral and kills her.

Llewelyn Moss

Llewelyn Moss is another central character of the novel. A Vietnam veteran and crackshot, Moss generates the action of the novel when he stumbles on more than two million dollars while hunting antelope. Though he is uneasy about his decision, Moss nevertheless takes the money and goes to great lengths to hide out from the men hired to get it back. Moss is an essentially honest man. He takes care of his wife and is well regarded by Bell and his deputies. Though he is a rough-hewn west Texas native with a code of honor closely resembling Sheriff Bell's, he cannot resist the allure of the found money and its imagined effects on his life. Moss's running battle with Anton Chigurh generates the main action of the novel.

Deputy Torbert

Another Terrell County deputy, Torbert is a minor character and works with Bell on the Moss-Chigurh case.

Carson Wells

An ex-U.S. Special Forces lieutenant colonel and former associate of Chigurh's, Wells is hired by the Matacumbe Petroleum group to kill Chigurh and recover the money for the drug-dealing syndicate. Wells first tracks Moss down at a Mexican hospital and warns him about Chigurh. Wells advises Moss to give back the money, explaining that this would protect not only Moss but also his wife Carla Jean. Moss refuses his help. Chigurh finds Wells in a hotel room and kills him.

Deputy Wendell

Wendell is a Terrell County deputy under the command of Sheriff Bell. He functions as Bell's right-hand man and is closely involved in the hunt for Moss and Chigurh.

Themes

Good and Evil

In the novel's first chapter, Bell recounts his visit to a man on death row. The man was convicted and sentenced to death, in a large part, due to Bell, who had arrested the murderer and testified at his trial. The man tells Bell that he had been planning on killing someone as long as he could remember and that he knew he was going to hell. Though a veteran sheriff, Bell is astounded. "I dont know what to make of that. I surely dont." It is Bell's next thought that sets the tone for the book's exploration of good and evil. Bell thinks "I thought I'd never seen a person like that and it got me to wonder in if maybe he was some new kind." This "new kind" takes the shape of ruthless killer Anton Chigurh in the subsequent chapter.

Bell is frightened by this new type of evil. He says that "Somewhere out there is a true and living prophet of destruction and I dont want to confront him. I know he's real. I have seen his work." For Bell, this fear is not about being older. He says "I think it is more about what you are will in to become." In other words, does good really triumph over evil if the good must become evil to fight the battle? As Bell puts it, "I think a man would have to put his soul at hazard. And I won't do that."

Based on Bell's thoughts in Chapter 1, the

novel can be read as an experiment in which this new kind of evil runs amok through a society that is not prepared to put its collective soul at hazard. Chigurh is not cut from the same cloth as Sheriff Bell, Llewelyn Moss, or even Carson Wells. Chigurh is free of the moral values shared by the other characters, and this freedom allows him to pursue Moss and the money with complete disregard for life, limb, and property.

Free Will and Determinism

What makes Chigurh so evil is his belief that events are predetermined. When he stops to put gas in a stolen car, he confronts the gas station owner and is willing to kill him based on the outcome of a coin toss. The owner is baffled by Chigurh, and Chigurh explains the role of the coin in the owner's fate. "It's been travelling twenty-two years to get here. And now it's here. And I'm here. And I've got my hand over it. And it's either heads or tails. And you have to say. Call it."

Chigurh sees himself simply as an instrument, and it is this detachment that makes him such a frightening and evil person. No other scene illustrates this as clearly as when Chigurh kills Carla Jean Moss. At this point in the novel, the money has been recovered; Chigurh has killed Moss; there is no logical reason that he must kill Carla Jean. But Chigurh has given his word to Moss that he would kill Carla Jean if Moss did not cooperate. And although Moss is dead, Chigurh says "But my word is not dead. Nothing can change that." In Chigurh's mind, Carla Jean was dead as soon as he promised Moss that he would kill her.

Carla Jean loses Chigurh's coin-flip game, and when she pleads for her life, he removes himself and sums up his philosophy.

> I had no say in the matter. Every moment in your life is a turning and every one a choosing. Somewhere you made a choice. All followed to this. The accounting is scrupulous. The shape is drawn. No line can be erased. I had no belief in your ability to move a coin to your bidding. How could you? A person's path through the world seldom changes and even more seldom will it change abruptly. And the shape of your path was visible from the beginning.

The novel's title is taken from Yeats's "Sailing to Byzantium." But for McCarthy, the "country" may be the America of the 1970s and 1980s, where the drug trade has redrawn the battle lines between good and evil. The bloody shootout over heroin and money in *No Country for Old Men* is the event that causes the paths of Moss, Bell, and Chigurh to intersect, and that presents McCarthy with the tools he needs to explore good, evil, and determinism.

Style

Readers will immediately notice that Cormac McCarthy's style and syntax are far from conventional. As a literary term *style* refers to a writer's personalized way of using sentence structure, figures of speech, diction, and other building blocks of the language. *Syntax* describes the way the author uses words to form phrases and sentences. In *No Country for Old Men*, McCarthy frequently omits commas, apostrophes, and several other punctuation marks. While his idiosyncratic style can make his writing more complicated to read at first, it does help McCarthy develop his characters and anchor the story's setting in the rural, desert region of southwest Texas.

Topics for Further Study

- Reread the sections of the novel that portray women. In what ways are Carla Jean Moss, Loretta Bell, and the hitchhiking woman similar? In what ways are the different? Choose a classmate and debate the following question: In *No Country for Old Men*, does McCarthy present women in a positive or negative light? Each of you choose a position and find passages in the text to support your conclusion.

- Watch the Coen brothers' film adaptation of *No Country for Old Men*. List three ways that the film is similar to McCarthy's novel. List three ways it is different. If you were selected to cast the film, what actors would you have chosen to play Moss, Bell, and Chigurh. Give a brief explanation of why the actors you chose would be right for their roles.

- Think of other crime stories or movies you have read or seen in recent years. What are some of the "classic" elements of the crime genre? Make a list of these elements and discuss which ones can be found in *No Country for Old Men*. How does the story fit into the genre as a whole? How is it different from the

Western genre Cormac McCarthy used in his previous books? Discuss why the author may have chosen this particular form of storytelling for this particular novel.

- McCarthy is very explicit in his descriptions of guns in *No Country for Old Men*. Choose one of these passages and explain how it is important to the mood or tone of the scene. Why do you think Chigurh uses the stun gun? What do you think the stun gun represents?

- Read the first several chapters of McCarthy's *Cities of the Plain*. How does the physical setting of that novel compare to the physical setting of *No Country for Old Men*? Examine three ways that John Grady Cole is similar to Sheriff Ed Tom Bell. How are the two characters different from the classic hero of the Western genre?

The novel begins with an *interior monologue*, a literary method of revealing a character's thoughts and emotions. McCarthy uses italics to show that these are the thoughts of Sheriff Ed Tom Bell. McCarthy also omits punctuation and uses unconventional spelling to replicate the sound of Bell's Texas dialect. "Said he knew he was go in to hell. Told it to me out of his own mouth. I dont know what to make of that. I surely dont."

No Country for Old Men is full of unusual spellings and written dialect. When Bell and Wendell investigate the scene of the shootout, Wendell asks, "The othern didnt have a gun?" Spelling "other one" as the contraction "othern" is typical of McCarthy's approach to written dialect.

McCarthy's syntax in *No Country for Old Men* also relies heavily on the word "and." He uses this conjunction frequently to string together short, independent phrases. In this passage, McCarthy describes Chigurh's actions:"He pulled in at the cafe and took the envelopes out of his shirtpocket and unfolded them and opened them and read the letters inside." The repeated use of "and" affects the pace of the narration. McCarthy frequently uses this type of construction when describing the actions of his characters.

No Country for Old Men fits into the crime fiction *genre*. A genre is a group of literary works that share similar characteristics and rely on certain *motifs*, or recurring elements. "Hard-boiled" actions or characters are characteristic of crime fiction. In this genre, "hard-boiled" describes the stoic toughness of a particular character or deed, and *No Country for Old Men* features some exceptionally hard-boiled people and scenes. The passage that depicts Chigurh cleaning and dressing his injured leg is classic hard-boiled crime fiction—the tough man, alone, painfully tending his bleeding wounds through gritted teeth. Llewelyn Moss is also a hard-boiled character. Though cautious, he is unfazed by the violence around him. McCarthy shows him unblinking and almost calm when he stumbles on the site of the shootout.

> Moss could see two clips sticking out of the canvas pocket of the jacket he was wearing. He reached into the cab and got them and stepped back. Smell of blood and fecal matter. He put one of the full clips into the machine-pistol and the other two in his pocket.

Throughout the novel, McCarthy is also meticulous in his description of the gun, a motif that runs throughout the story. When Moss is hunting antelope in the beginning of the novel, we learn that the rifle is "a heavy barreled .270 on a '98 Mauser action." Bell says that he prefers the old "Colts .44-40," and nearly every chapter has a description of a gun, bullet hole, or ammunition. The closely linked motifs of guns and hard-boiled descriptions put *No Country for Old Men* squarely in the crime genre.

The Rural Southwest

In 1976 Cormac McCarthy moved to El Paso, Texas, a region that has had a profound impact on his writing. The Chihuahuan Desert that covers northern Mexico and portions of Texas, New Mexico, and Arizona provides the backdrop for *Blood Meridian* and the three novels of the Border Trilogy, as well as for *No Country for Old Men*.

In *No Country for Old Men* McCarthy puts the lives and culture of the rural Southwestern denizens squarely in the path of the border drug-smuggling business. While the events of the novel occur in 1980, McCarthy uses Ed Tom Bell's interior monologues to express a former time's sense of values—one that is unaccustomed to the violence of modern America. Bell is dismayed by what he reads in the papers: killing sprees, mothers who murder their children, teenagers with green hair and nose rings. In one telling passage, Bell remembers attending a conference in Corpus Christi where he met a woman who did not share his, or his peoples', values:

> And she kept talk in about the right
> wing this and the right wing that. I
> aint even sure what she meant by it.
> The people I know are mostly just
> common people. Common as dirt, as

the sayin goes. I told her that and she looked at me funny. She thought I was sayin somethin bad about em, but of course that's a high compliment in my part of the world. She kept on, kept on. Finally told me, said: I dont like the way this country is headed. I want my granddaughter to be able to have an abortion.

Richard Woodward writes in his 1992 *New York Times* interview with the author that "McCarthy doesn't write about places he hasn't visited, and he has made dozens of similar scouting forays to Texas, New Mexico, Arizona, and across the Rio Grande into Chihuahua, Sonora, and Coahuila." For McCarthy, west Texas in 1980 is a physical place but also a state of mind. He uses Bell and his stream-of-consciousness passages to give the reader a sense of how the people of that time and place felt.

Border Drug Trafficking

Crashing into this rural southwestern ethos is the violence of the international drug-smuggling business. Drug smuggling across the Texas—Mexico border could be a particularly bloody affair. The violence that accompanied the bustling drug trade was shocking. During the 1980s, Pablo Escobar's Medellin drug cartel was a major player in the black market for drugs. Escobar's widespread power was noteworthy, but it was the violence associated with his cartel that was frequently in the news. In *The Culture of Violence*, Kumar Rupesinghe describes the savage scope of the drug trade. "The violence escalated in 1983 when Rodrigo Lara Bonilla, the Minister of Justice, was assassinated, and it continued to worsen until February 1991. At its peak, as many as 100 policemen were killed in one month."

Two clues in the novel reveal that McCarthy had a real historical model in mind when writing *No Country for Old Men*. Though his name is never mentioned fully (characters use only his last name and first name in different parts of the text), Pablo Acosta is the drug cartel leader that pursues Moss in the novel. Throughout the 1970s and 1980s, Acosta gained the status as a hyper-violent outlaw, and it is this level of drug-related violence that provides the context for the violence of the book. In keeping with the theme of a new kind of evil, Sheriff Bell wonders about this modern breed of criminal. "I aint sure we've seen these people before. Their kind. I dont know what to do about em even. If you killed em all they'd have to build an annex on to hell."

Winding through the novel is Anton Chigurh and his unspeakable acts of violence against the people of the region. In some ways, the shocking violence of the drug-running trade is distilled down into Anton Chigurh. The lengths he goes to recover the money—the garrote, the gun, the cattle prod, the car bomb—are a sort of catalog of the atrocities that the Medellin cartel and Acosta's crew committed throughout the period.

Critical Overview

Widely considered a virtuoso, Cormac McCarthy received generally positive feedback from the newspapers, magazines, and journals that reviewed *No Country for Old Men*. Many reviewers focus on McCarthy's treatment of the crime fiction genre. In the *New York Times* Walter Kirn called the book "as bracing a variation on these noir orthodoxies as any fan of the genre could expect." Critics were generally content with the way that McCarthy handled the hard-boiled characters, gunplay, and violence that are the hallmarks of crime fiction. McCarthy, however, was taken to task for his depiction of women in the novel. For example, Salon.com's Ira Boudway critiqued McCarthy's characters' "crusty machismo."

Another focal point for critics and reviewers was McCarthy's unconventional style. Jeffrey Lent, writing for the *Washington Post*, said that "McCarthy's language is stripped lean and mean here. In places, dialogue carries large sections of the story. His ear for speech, dialect and wordplay remains noteworthy in American letters." While the majority of readers and critics were impressed by the author's command of the language, there were some reviewers that thought that McCarthy's unconventional spelling and lack of punctuation was indulgent and confusing to the reader.

McCarthy's novels have always attempted to

put forth a worldview or philosophy, and *No Country for Old Men* is no exception. In McCarthy's books, there is always a higher power in play. As Jack Sexton sums up in the journal *Quadrant*: In all his books, God is neither personal nor loving. But nor is He dead. Instead, He and his purposes are so unspeakably alien to humankind that to speak of Him as caring or as not caring for us, His creatures, is senseless.

What Do I Read Next?

- *Blood Meridian* (1985) is often ranked as Cormac McCarthy's best novel. The book traces the life of "the kid," a Tennessee teenager who comes to Texas and joins up with a gang of scalp hunters. *Blood Meridian* is a complicated and violent story, with dense philosophical passages and a number of scenes that feature incredible violence and depravity. It is McCarthy's fifth book and his first novel set in the Southwest.

- *All the Pretty Horses* (1992) is a coming-of-age story set along the Texas-Mexico border. Far more romantic than the vision of the West supplied by *Blood Meridian*, *All the Pretty Horses* tells the story of John Grady Cole and his friend Lacey Rawlins and their move from America to Mexico.

- *The Crossing* (1994) is the second book of McCarthy's heralded border trilogy. The novel is set in the Southwest just before the outbreak of World War II. It chronicles Billy and Boyd Parham's journey to Mexico and back. The tone of the novel is a continuation of the more nostalgic tone that McCarthy used in *All the Pretty Horses*.

- *Cities of the Plain* (1998) is the final book in the border trilogy. The novel brings together the characters of John Grady Cole from *All the Pretty Horses* and Billy Parham from *The Crossing*. While working together at a ranch in New Mexico, John Grady falls in love with a young Mexican prostitute and vows to marry her and free her from her enslavement. John Grady is killed by the prostitute's vicious pimp, and the novel skips ahead to an elderly Billy and his attempts to make his way in a rapidly changing world.

- *Riders of the Purple Sage* (1912), by Zane Grey, is one of the quintessential novels of the Western genre. The novel lays out many of the motifs of the Western, including a moral code based on personal honor and the wide-open geographical space of the Western United States.

- *Perspectives on Cormac McCarthy* (1993), edited by Edwin T. Arnold and Dianne C. Luce, provides a good overview of the author's work and comprises more than two hundred pages of essays about McCarthy's novels.

Sources

Boudway, Ira, *Powell's Books*, August 26, 2005, from www.powells.com/review/2005_08_26

Kirn, Walter, *The New York Times*, July 24, 2005, from www.nytimes.com/2005/07/24/books/review/24KIR

Lent, Jeffrey, *The Washington Post*, July 17, 2005, from www.washingtonpost.com/wp-dyn/content/article/2005/07/15/AR2005071500732.h

McCarthy, Cormac, *No Country for Old Men*, Alfred A. Knopf, 2005.

Rupesinghe, Kumar, *The Culture of Violence*, United Nations University Press, 1994, p. 99.

Sexton, Jack, "The Natural Weight of Words," in *Quadrant*, November 2005, pp. 86–87.

Simmon, Scott, *The Invention of the Western Film*, Cambridge University Press, 2003, p. 127.

Woodward, Richard B., *The New York Times on the Web*, April 19, 1992, www.nytimes.com/books/98/05/17/specials/mccarth venom.html

Further Reading

Arnold, Edwin T. and Diane C. Luce, *A Cormac McCarthy Companion: The Border Trilogy*, University Press of Mississippi, 2001.

> This collection of essays explores the Border Trilogy and unearths some of the books' deeper themes, including war, dreams, and evolution.

McCarthy, Cormac, *Blood Meridian*, Random House Modern Library Edition, 2001.

> Readers unfamiliar with McCarthy's novels can compare and contrast the dense, complicated language of *Blood Meridian* with the relatively sparse prose of *No Country for Old Men*.

Thompson, Jim, *Savage Night*, Vintage, 1997.

> Thompson's novel is one of the classics of the crime fiction genre. While the book explores different themes than the ones McCarthy investigates in *No Country for Old Men*, it does feature hard-boiled characters and a first-person narrator, which may draw some comparisons to Sheriff Ed Tom Bell's stream-of-consciousness meditations.

Woodward, Richard B., "Cormac McCarthy's

Venomous Fiction," *The New York Times*, April 1992, Sunday Late Edition.

> Based on an extensive interview with the author, the article provides a good introduction to McCarthy and the themes and styles in his writing.